THE HAND BOOK OF SWINDLING

Curious
PUBLICATIONS

New York

Published by Curious Publications
101 W. 23rd St. #318
New York, NY 10011
curiouspublications.com

ISBN-13: 979-8-9864760-5-6

The Hand-Book of Swindling was originally published by
Chapman and Hall in 1839. The cover art is from that edition.

Printed and bound in the United States of America.

Original ad, published in the Essex County Standard, *October 25, 1839.*

Barnabas Whitefeather

THE

HAND-BOOK OF SWINDLING.

BY THE LATE

CAPTAIN BARABBAS WHITEFEATHER,

LATE OF THE BODY-GUARD OF HIS MAJESTY, KING CARLOS ; TREASURER
OF THE BRITISH WINE AND VINEGAR COMPANY ; TRUSTEE FOR
THE PROTECTION OF THE RIVER THAMES FROM INCEN-
DIARIES ; PRINCIPAL INVENTOR OF POYAIS STOCK ;
RANGER OF ST. GEORGE'S FIELDS ; ORIGINAL
PATENTEE OF THE PARACHUTE CON-
VEYANCE ASSOCIATION ; KNIGHT
OF EVERY ORDER OF
THE FLEECE ;
SCAMP
AND
CU
R

" A man he was to all the country *dear*."—GOLDSMITH.

EDITED BY JOHN JACKDAW.

WITH ILLUSTRATIONS

BY

PHIZ

LONDON :

CHAPMAN AND HALL, 186, STRAND.

MDCCCXXXIX.

PREFACE OF THE EDITOR

THE Editor has disciplined himself to receive with becoming moderation the tremendous expression of national gratitude consequent on the publication of this valuable work—the production of the late estimable CAPTAIN BARABBAS WHITEFEATHER. It was discovered among many other papers accidentally left at the lodgings of the deceased, and placed in the hands of the editor by the executors of the lamented and—if a novel epithet may be applied to him—talented author.

When "HAND-BOOKS" devoted to the lighter elegancies, nay, to the frivolities, of life are every day poured down upon a thankful generation, it would indeed be to incur the charge of poltroonery to doubt the brilliant success of the present essay.

The philosophical observer who has witnessed the fervent welcome accorded by a British public to "THE HANDBOOK OF SKITTLES," "THE HANDBOOK OF

Cheese-Toasting," "The Handbook of Eel-Skin-ning," "The Handbook of Nutmeg-Grating," "The Handbook of Corn-Cutting," "The Handbook of Kitten-Drowning," and other productions of lesser pith and purpose,—the philosophic observer cannot but glow with the sweetest and liveliest feelings of anticipated pleasure at the outburst of national gratitude acknowledging and rejoicing in the publication of

"The Hand-book of Swindling."

Let us for a moment consider the comprehensiveness of the subject. Other Hand-Books have their merits and their uses: far be it from the editor to detract one iota from their claims upon a thoughtful people; yet it must be conceded that their different subjects apply rather to the wants of sections of the public than to the public in its integrity. For instance, how few rejoice in the masculine exercise of skittles! Toasted cheese, albeit the favourite diet of many of Cyclopean digestion, is sedulously shunned by dyspeptic hundreds of thousands. The class of the eel-skinning public is indeed most limited; nutmeg is never dreamt of by at least a million of our fellow-subjects; a million more, it is our cheerful hope, know not the visitation of corns; whilst, could a census be taken of the number of kittens annually sacrificed by drowning, it would possibly be discovered that not one British subject out of five hundred is ever called upon to perform that painful, yet necessary and most domestic operation. It must then be acknowledged that all handbooks hitherto published are more or less limited in their application; but for "THE HAND-BOOK OF SWINDLING,"—why, it is a national work; a *vade mecum* for a whole people!

It was the intention of the editor to dedicate this work to some illustrious individual worthy of the distinction. But so many candidates—all equally deserving of the honour—with claims so nicely balanced, rose before him, that the editor, considering it would be invidious to many to select one alone, dedicates the book to the nation at large. Yes, he gives it to his country; but too well repaid if he shall be the means of calling from the working day road of life one simple traveller to the pleasant "primrose path" made easier and laid more open to him by this golden volume.

BREAKNECK STEPS,
    OLD BAILEY.

THE
HAND-BOOK OF SWINDLING

CHAPTER I

THE READER IS INTRODUCED TO CAPTAIN
WHITEFEATHER'S RELATIONS

IT was a favourite conviction of my late respected uncle and godfather, Barabbas Whitefeather— he fell in the very flower of his age, at only forty-five, a premature victim to the insalubrity of Bermuda, where he was stationed in a very public capacity by the British Government—it was, I say, a pet belief of the sagacious Barabbas that every man had within him what I think heathen philosophers have called a particle of divine gold; but which my uncle, in the fine simplicity of his nature, and at the same time humanely accommodating his language to the lowest understanding of his species, denominated "a bit of the swindler."

Discriminating reader, Barabbas Whitefeather was a man of homespun wit, who chewed not his words until they had lost all their original form and vigour; no, he flung them from him with the air of a man who knows he is laying down a guinea of the best mint gold, and not timidly and sneakingly, like a passer of gilt copper.

"Every man has within him a bit of the swindler!"

The sentence fell upon me in the days of my earliest childhood; yes, it was in that ductile, happy, and susceptible season of life that the words of my uncle Barabbas—precious seed!—dropped into my infant heart, where—but let me not boast, let me rather indulge in the luxury of memory—yes, suffer me, complying reader, to carry you into the presence of my sainted uncle: bear with me whilst with affectionate reverence I call up from the abyss of time the interesting shadow of Barabbas Whitefeather.

It was my birthday—I was six years old. I had been promised that that day should be distinguished by a circumstance which, as we advance in life and become involved in the meshes of the world, is apt to be forgotten, albeit of the first importance at the time—I was to be breeched. *I was not.* I can only remember that a cloud seemed suddenly to have fallen upon our house—that my father would come home long after the lamb had lain down to rest, and would still leave the domestic roof before the rising of the lark, that his temper, generally rough, became much rougher; and that, only a few days before my birthday, on expressing my infantine delights at the trumpets blown before the newly-arrived judges, he rebuked me with unwonted emphasis, at the same time wishing the trumpets and the judges, as I then conceived, very oddly incorporated with one another. I was then within a few days of six years old—I was a fine, tall, plump child, and on my birthday was to have been breeched. The neighbourhood called for it. I repeat it, my birthday came and passed, and found and left me still in coats.

That day, however, was ordained to be the most eventful of my life. It is that day which, if the world shall continue to remember the deeds of Captain Barabbas Whitefeather, must be held by posterity in especial respect. It is to that day that I owe everything; and what I owe, it would be the worst of affectation in the world to deny or to forget. To proceed with my history.

"Brab,"—it was thus my father was wont to tamper with the euphony of Barabbas,—"Brab, nunkey wants to see you; so you must toddle with me."

Some weeks had elapsed since I had seen uncle Barabbas; and at his name visions of cakes and apples, peg-tops and whipping-tops, rose before me. Like Agesilaus, Socrates, Yorick, and other men whom I do not hesitate to call of his kidney, my uncle would chequer and ameliorate the labour of public life by sporting with little children. "He hath borne me on his back a thousand times." I was of course delighted at the prospect of visiting my uncle; but was at the same time made to wonder at the preparation of my father, who carefully bound up one of his eyes, glued large whiskers on his cheeks, and otherwise so disguised himself that, although I saw him do it, I could scarcely believe it was he. However, I thought it was all to have some game with Uncle Barabbas—and in my childishness crowed with laughter at anticipation of the sport.

I walked with my father, and in about half-an-hour came to a very large house, a place I had never seen before: for my dear mother, always fuming about fevers and measles, kept me close at home. My father, suddenly walking very lame, knocked at the door, and through a cold that had come on him all in a minute, asked hoarsely enough for my uncle. The man let us in, and then another man went before us; and then I knew I was in a place where there were heaps of gold and diamonds, for the man unlocked and locked again at least a dozen doors. I give my childish impressions, which I entreat the reader not to smile at, but to remember the simplicity and ingenuousness of my age. Well, after a time, we were led into an open court, where some gentlemen were throwing up halfpence, and two on a bench were pushing straws; and there was one dancing,

Philosophy in Stone Walls

and one or two singing, and all as happy as birds.

I looked round the place and saw uncle Barabbas smoking in a corner. I was about to call him when my father gave my arm such a pull I thought it was broken; and so I resolved to say nothing, but to wait and see the fun that father would play off upon uncle. Sure enough Barabbas never knew him; and though my uncle patted me upon the head, he had, I thought, forgotten me, for he gave me nothing. My father and my uncle talked together for a long time; when—I see my uncle now— Barabbas suddenly brought himself up, and raising his head, and extending his right arm, the palm open, he said in a solemn voice:—

"Depend upon it, every man has within him a bit of the swindler."

My father shook his head; whereupon my uncle, for he was very scholarly, and could talk for an hour without stopping, proceeded as follows:—I am perfectly certain as to the words, having subsequently found the whole written speech among other of my uncle's papers; Barabbas, like some other wits and orators, carefully putting in pen and ink any brilliant thought that struck him—any argument that was a hobby with him, that he might at proper season extemporaneously bring it forth to the delight and astonishment of his hearers. My father shook his head at the dogma of my uncle, who, without stop, continued:—

"Are you so ignorant as to believe in the deficiency of mankind in general—to imagine that nature is so partial a mother as to dower with her best gifts only a few of her children, leaving the multitude defence-less, unarmed? My dear sir,"—here my uncle lowered his voice,—"amend your ignorance—be just to nature. Do you see tigers whelped without claws—elephants calved that never have tusks—rattlesnakes hatched with no stings? Is nature so niggard—so partial—so unjust? No—philosophers and conquerors have made their marks, and signed their names to the fact—to swindle is to exhibit the peculiar attribute of the human ani-mal; it is at once the triumph and distinguishing faculty of the race. But you will say, do all men swindle? and I ask, do all snakes sting—all elephants gore? There is, however, an unanswerable argument which proves that men, when gregarious, are inevitably swindlers; at least, if they are not, let not the failing be placed to their account; they would be, if they might. Let me put a case. You recollect Gloss, the retired merchant? What an excellent man was Gloss! A pattern man to make a whole generation by! Nobody could surpass him in what is called honesty, rectitude, moral propri-ety, and other gibberish. Well, Gloss joins a 'Board'; he becomes one of a community; and, immediately, the latent feeling asserts itself: he is a backbone man with the rest of his brotherhood; and though as simple

Gloss, and not a member of the 'board,' he is the same as ever, yet when acting with his fellows, when one of the body corporate, when he merges the man Gloss in the board member, the inherent faculty becomes active, and he gratifies the instinct, or the refined reason, or whatever men agree to call it—and complacently swindles with the rest. He cannot do otherwise: human nature is tested by the occasion; and if, under the circumstances, he refuse to swindle, he ceases to be a man. Swindling, my dear sir"—and here my uncle spoke in a tremulous voice, and my father seemed touched by the emotion—"Swindling, my dear sir, has indeed a far more comprehensive meaning than that superficially awarded to it by, possibly, very respectable people. Good soldiers may fight, pillage, and violate under a banner, and yet, in truth, shall not be able to read and interpret the legend emblazoned on it."

I could perceive that my father did not perfectly understand this. He, therefore, nodded assentingly, and my uncle, with new animation, proceeded:—

"When I reflect on the extensive and subtle operation of the faculty—when I perceive that, in this our best possible social state, it is, so to speak, the cement that keeps society together; the bond of union; the very salt of human government—it does, I confess it, irk me to find men ungraciously deny its existence, putting off its triumphs upon other motives, and depriv-

ing swindling of the glory of its deeds. Strange per-
version of human intellect—laughable contradiction
of moral purposes! Thus, the politician flutters at the
very breath of swindler; thus, the stockbroker struts
and swells, and lays his hand upon his waistcoat with
a blank look of wondering innocence at the slightest
allusion to the faculty that makes a man of him—to
which he owes his carriage and country house, his con-
servatories and his pineries; and above all, the flattering
hope of calling Lord Giggleton son-in-law; his lordship
being over head, and, what is more, over ears in love
with Arabella's guineas. And yet, such is the base, the
black ingratitude of human nature, that this man, this
most adroit and lucky stockbroker, starts even at the
name of swindler! He indignantly denies the slightest
obligation to the higher faculty—the *mens divinior* of
the cabinet, the mart, and the counting-house. Look at
Sir Godfrey Measles, the illustrious pork contractor, in
whom our brave and magnanimous sailors confide for
dinners. Did he not in the most handsome way forfeit a
fine to his king and country for having failed to supply
swine's flesh at so much per stone? And then, having
paid his fine like a patriot and a man,—did he not, having before bought up all the pork to be had—did he
not, with the gushing feelings of a philanthropist, offer
it at three times the contract price? Now what was this?
Men who veil their meaning in allegory may say that

Sir Godfrey Measles 'drove his pigs to a fine market.'
For myself, I elevate the homely phrase of pig-driver
into the more ennobling name of swindler. Others may
say that Sir Godfrey only traded—I stick to my belief;
I say he swindled. More: I reverence him for the act;
my only deep regret is, that he should have failed in an
ingenuous gratitude, and denied the action of the higher principle. I have long looked upon the world, and,
with sorrow, I say it, in nothing do the generations of
successful men show so much cold and callous ingratitude as in their treatment of their guardian genius, that
prettiest of Pucks, that best of Robin Goodfellows, that
deftest of household fairies, hight Swindling!"

My father cast his one eye towards his eloquent
brother with a look of speaking admiration; and, although there was a pause, did not presume to make
any rejoinder. My uncle proceeded:—

"But why number examples? Why attempt to
prove that which every man, if he would but consult
the recesses of his own bosom, must truly know? Ask
all the professions; demand of the lawyer, with yellow,
studious cheek, wherefore he should coin gold out of
little strips of paper, written over by youthful scribes
at two or three shillings per diem. Request him to give
you the philosophy of costs—the exquisite meaning of
appearance and declaration, and reply and rejoinder,
and all the thousand terms invented by the most cun-

ning class of labourers, the overlookers at the building
of Babel. Ask the sleek practitioner to what he owes his
fortune. To common-sense—to justice—to the fair and
rational barter of labour for shillings? If he be a hypo-
crite—if he be resolved to clap in with the world, and
carry on a profitable duplicity, he will swell like a bull-
frog at the query, and, forgetful of his knuckles, will
strike his heart, answering with the big-mouthed 'Yes!'
But if at the end of a long practice there should by miracle remain in that attorney's bosom a throb of truth,
he will blandly, yet significantly smile at the words—the
counters men play with—common-sense and justice,
and magnanimously and unblushingly declare his debt
to—swindling!

"Is it otherwise with the physician, who sells his
guesses for truth, and doubts and doubts a patient into
the grave, whilst his medicinal palm is open for the
guinea? When the apothecary vends cinnamon and
peppermint water for *elixir vitæ*, doth he practise a noble art? Yea; for, safely and successfully, he—swindles.

"When the tradesman—his housemaid at the time
perhaps in Bridewell for petty larceny committed on
the greasepot—when he, smiling across the counter
at his victim, puts off knowingly the poorest commodity at the highest price, how stands he in relation to
his captive handmaid? Why, Rebecca has robbed, but
the tradesman has only driven his trade: the slut has

for ever and for ever lost her character, with it seven pounds *per annum*, and, it may be, tea and sugar included—but for Mr Jackson, her master, he has turned the profit penny; he has—but all in the way of business—swindled."

"It is very true," exclaimed my father with an oath, "it is very true. When what is swindling isn't swindling according to law, it's a fortune to a man; but when it's agin law, and found out——"

"The result I know," cried my uncle, a slight tint of red suffusing his manly cheek. "All mankind may be divided into two classes: the swindlers according to custom and to law, and the swindlers according to the bent of their natural genius."

"True agin," cried my father, slapping his thigh.

"Still, the propensity," said my uncle, "is universal: men only want temptation. It is extraordinary how, like a chain, the feeling runs from breast to breast. Jack Smasher was one of the prettiest hands at coining; and more, he was blessed with a wife born, I should say, with a genius for passing bad money. She took a crown—one of her husband's base-begotten offspring—purchased with it three pennyworth of rhubarb from a Quaker chemist, who—undone man!—handed over four-and-ninepence change. Aminadab Straightback was, even among his brethren, the brightest child of truth. In due season Aminadab detected the guileful crown, and in his own clear breast resolved to destroy it. However, it remained by the strangest accident in his till, and by an accident still more extraordinary, was given in part of change for a guinea to a gentleman a little the worse for liquor, who on his way home to bed took the precaution of dropping into Straightback's for a box of— his own patent—anti-bacchic pills. In the morning the vinous gentleman discovered the pocket-piece, but as he had changed more than one guinea, could not with certainty detect the giver of the counterfeit. No matter. It remained loose with other money in his pocket, and one day, to his own surprise, he found he had passed it. He had taken a journey, and it was very dark when, in the handsomest manner, he fee'd the coachman. The poor man who drove the Tally-ho did not realise more than £400 per annum, and could not afford to lose five shillings; hence Smasher's crown became at a fitting opportunity the property of a sand-blind old gentlewoman, who, her loss discovered, lifted up her hands at the iniquity of the world, and put aside the brassy wickedness. The good old soul never missed a charity sermon. The Reverend Mr Sulphurtongue made a sweet discourse in favour of the conversion of the Jews, and the churchwardens condescended to hold each a plate. To the great disgust of the discoverers, a bad crown was detected amongst the subscribed half-crowns and shillings. The beadle was directed to destroy it. He intended to do so, but, in pure forgetfulness, passed it one day for purl; the landlady of the 'George' having, as she said 'taken it, was resolved not to lose it,' and by some accident it was given to a pedlar, who, after a walk of twenty miles, entered an ale-house, took his supper of bread and cheese, went to bed, rose, and proffered for his account Jack Smasher's pocket-piece. The pedlar was immediately given into the hands of a constable, taken before a magistrate, and ordered to be imprisoned and whipped as a passer of counterfeit coin."

"See what luck is!" cried my father; "it's the Quaker *what* should have lost the dollar."

"He couldn't do it; for though he was a most respectable person, and lived and died with that character, he was but a man. He had been swindled—the link of the chain was touched, and it vibrated—you perceive, it vibrated?"

Again my father nodded.

"Yes," exclaimed Barabbas Whitefeather, "I repeat it—the sympathy is universal. All men can, do, or might, swindle. Though with many the propensity be latent, it surely exists, and needs but the happy moment to be awakened into life. The proof is easy: take ten, twenty, thirty men—creatures of light; admirable, estimable, conscientious persons; by-words of excellence, proverbs of truth in their individual dealings; and yet,

make of them a 'board'—a 'committee'—a 'council'—a 'company'—no matter what may be the collective name by which they may be known—and immediately every member will acknowledge the quickening
of a feeling—a sudden growth of an indomitable lust
to—swindle. What is this but a proof of the faculty—as
I have said—dormant, but requiring only the necessary
agent to awaken it? Oh! let no man perk himself up in
the pride of his innocence—strut and pout, big with
the prejudice of respectability! He knows not the mys-
tery of his own nature; for though to his own eyes he
shall be a saint, he will, when time and purpose shall
see fit to call his better feelings into life, he will, he must,
he cannot do otherwise than—swindle."

My father, though a strong man, was much affected.

"As for you, my dear child," said my uncle, taking
me by the hand, kissing me, and looking benevolently
upon me, "as for you, remember the words of Barabbas
Whitefeather. At present you know not their worth, but
a time will come when better than pearls or gold will
be this my parting council to you. Throughout your life
do nought but swindle. If you can, swindle on the right
side of the statute, but at all events, my dear child,"—
even now I feel the pressure of that wise man's lip, the
warm tear trickling down my cheeks, "at all events,
Barabbas, swindle!"

I am now in my nine-and-thirtieth year; and from

my first day of discretion until this, the season of ripest manhood, I can, laying my hand upon my heart, most conscientiously declare that never for a moment have I forgotten the last injunction of the best of uncles. But why should I speak on this head? The world will do me justice.

My uncle shook my parent by the hand. "Good-bye," he said; "we may never meet again, for I am now two-and-forty, and you know"—this I could *not* understand—"you know *it's fourteen penn'orth.*"

My father, choking with emotion, cried, "D—n 'em!" We quitted my uncle; and I trust I shall not be accused of adopting the language of hyperbole, when I state that we quitted him with feelings far more easy of conception than description.

Only a twelvemonth after this, I lost my excellent father. It may prove to the giddy and the vain the uncertainty of life, when I state that my worthy parent was in robust health one minute and dead the next. It may also prove that he had held some place in the world, when I assure the reader that crowds of people flocked to our house to pay honour to his cold remains; which, for the benefit of his widow and son, were exhibited at sixpence a head to grown persons, and half-price for children. I should be unjust to my parent's memory were I to withhold another circumstance illustrative of the consequence of my father to the world at large: the night-cap in which he died was purchased by a gentleman, a lover of the fine arts, after a severe contest with other bidders, for two guineas.

And so much for my uncle and my father, both worthy of the name of Whitefeather.

CHAPTER II

No—the theme is too pregnant with circumstance; too
vast—too voluminous. Let me then subdue the vain,
though laudable, ambition—let me repress the fond,
the wild desire of such distinction. Is it for a single pen
to write the History of Swindling? Is it for one man to
chronicle, with scrupulous fidelity, the rise and progress
of the exquisite art (for I must call it so)? Is it for one
curious pair of eyes—one toilsome hand—to pore over
and put down the many million facts to be registered
in a complete body of the Science? Could the life of a
patriarch, even though he worked the hours of a cot-
ton-spinner, suffice for the labour? Consider, Barabbas,
what running to and fro—what fetching and carrying
of truths—what sifting and winnowing of chaff and
husk—what gold-washing—what pearl-diving! Now

picking up stray matter for your work in Egypt—now, with a thought, among the sages in India—now off, it may be, upon a wild-goose chase to Arabia Petræa— now among the Scandinavians—and now, cold as a snowball, to be called away to the opium-sellers at the walls of the Tartars! Is it possible for one man, though with ribs of brass and soles of adamant, to go through the toil and travel? And this, be it remarked, will only take in the first thousand years or so of the age of our dear, ill-used mother earth. How much remains to be done—what crooked ways to thread—what dirt and rust to scratch away—what inscriptions to guess at— what monuments to measure—even before you come to Semiramis! And when, reeling like a porter under a thousand-weight of facts—for a very few facts make a pound—you arrive at Semiramis, have you disciplined yourself to bear the indifference of a superficial gen- eration—to be askcd by listless ignorance, "Who the devil is Semiramis?" Dear Barabbas, your yearnings are indeed most noble; but there is a limit to human ac- tion—there is a point where man must stop. The task is not earthly; or, if indeed it be a mortal labour, it is only to be achieved by the united heads and hands of many. A band of hard-working encyclopædists—temperate labourers living upon bread and water and figs—might possibly, in the course of a few lustres, produce some hundred volumes of the work; but a complete body of swindling from the birth of time to its present lust-ihood, it is a thing only to be dreamed of—a glorious phantasm—a magnificent but most deceitful vision!

But grant it done. Say that the last proof—the ten millionth sheet—lies before you, the smooth-faced dev-il waiting at your garret door to carry off the corrected matter for the press. Say that it is printed, published, and the whole five hundred volumes folio scrupulously conned, as they doubtless would be, by the critics—alack! alack!—what a melancholy book hath the press groaned with—what a ghastly chronicle, what a blood-dyed, tear-stained record!

"A complete body of swindling!" Let us turn a few of the leaves. They creak like dungeon hinges! Are not the pictures terrible? Whole generations of men, thin-chapped, hollow-eyed, scourged and in bonds; fainting in midday; stark with the dews of night. Tens of thou-sands, living carcasses, in mines—thousands and thou-sands writhing in blood and agony upon the field—with the vassals of glory, a cloud of vultures, hovering to pick their bones. Next let us peep through prison bars, and—no; close the book—it is too shocking—one's marrow freezes, and the brain reels at it.

"Methinks," says the reader, "the Captain takes a too comprehensive view of his subject."

Right, sagacious reader; and yet, were the history of swindling in all its ramifications to be duly chronicled, the work would be no less voluminous, no jot less tragical. The present is, after all, not an auspicious age for folios; neither is it the best of all possible eras for the publication of disagreeable truths. Lazarus himself, to touch worldly sympathy, should in these days be a Lazarus in superfine cloth—the best cambric and the glossiest beaver; nay, he would be something the gainer by a waistcoat of gold-smeared velvet, and, at least, a chain of silver. To make iniquity or sorrow bearable, it is highly necessary that it should be properly dressed. Hence, reader, I, Barabbas Whitefeather, instructed by the better spirit of the age, forego my first Utopian purpose, and leaving the full history of swindling to be written by a future college of sages, shall confine myself more immediately to the existing wants of the world—shall attend to the crying necessities of the present generation. Controlled by my better genius, I renounce folios.

After all, the world has not, as I at first superficially believed, so keen a want of a complete history of swindling: for how many books have been written which, although not professedly treating of the theme, are, by their very subject, works of reference and authority in the matter! What, for instance, is much of *Ancient Histor*? What *The Lives of the Roman Emperors*? What *The History of Conquests*? What *The History of Discovery*—from the first finding of Mesopotamia to the last providential flight upon New Zealand? If men will read not with their eyes alone, but with understanding hearts, how much is there in all these works, in all these narratives, that is indeed no other than materials for a complete body of swindling? Loose pearls that need stringing—scattered lights to be brought to one point? Indeed, to a contemplative mind, to a reader properly prepared for the perusal of history and biography, it is almost impossible for him to open a volume from which he should not gather knowledge of a swindling kind. It is often the very staple of a book, though to the shame of many writers, I grieve to say it, the subject is most ungenerously disguised under foreign trappings—passed off under a false name. Hence, reflecting that if men will look round them, they are not wholly destitute of works containing the philosophy of swindling on a grand historical scale—on an enlarged and transcendental plan—I shall endeavour to prevail upon myself to become merely useful, leaving it to the poorly ambitious to glitter and to soar. Let other men make pedestals to themselves of unopened folios; they have their veneration—they are talked of, never read. I—I will descend among the crowd—will mix with my fellow-creatures—will right and left scatter among the children of innocence a "Handbook"—a veritable tome to be carried between the thumbs and fingers of men in their paths by day, and like a guardian and protecting genius to nestle in their bosoms at night. Yes, it shall be no large carcass of a book; no literary mammoth of a bygone time; a load for a shelf; but a light and dainty fairy for the palm. A "Handbook!"— Yes, there is a freshness, a beauty, a truthfulness in the name; it shall be "THE HAND-BOOK OF SWINDLING." Uncut folios, avaunt! and, thick as humming-birds in tropic groves, "Handbooks," in green and gold, trim your glowing winglets and flutter among men.[1]

Having resolved upon the mode in which I shall benefit humanity, having come to the determination to contract myself into the smallest possible size, that I may the more deftly make my way among the crowd, it is but due to myself—it is but just to my readers—to make known in a few words the extent and range of my purpose. That purpose is, I am proud to feel it, of the best wisdom, of the noblest benevolence; it is to make every man—at least every thinking, reasonable man, for I write not to blockheads—a SWINDLER. Yes; it is my aim to render him, at all points, armed for the contest

1 The reader will perceive from the self-complacency with which the author talks of "Handbook," that he would pass the compound as purely one of his own invention. The editor, however, conceives it to be a part of his stern duty to state that a book printed at Baden-Baden, where the Captain was wont to retire in autumn for the benefit of the waters and other benefits—a book entitled (we give the English) "The Handbook of Cogging," was found among the Captain's other literary effects. He had, doubtless, forgotten that *Hand-Book* was from *Hand-Buch*.—[Ed.]

of life—to prepare him for the cutting and thrusting and picking and stealing of this eventful passage. It is my purpose to make known a few golden rules—the result of a long and various experience—by which the attentive and quick-witted student may learn to play with men as he would play with pieces of chess, by which every move on the board of life may be his own, to the utter discomfiture of a plodding and merely painstaking opponent. And in all this there shall be nothing legally forbidden; nothing that shall suddenly shock your delicate nostrils, reader, with the smell of hemp: no, no; though turnkeys and the hangman walk about you, if you are an apt scholar, you shall snap your fingers at them, and swindle securely.

"And now," thinks the reader,—for I know his thoughts as well as I know my own whiskers,—"now the book begins to open; now the work warms up." Be not impatient.

Impressed as I am with the purpose of this inestimable little work, it befits the dignity of that purpose that there should be no unseemly haste, no helter-skelter in the communication of ideas. Were I writing the "HAND-BOOK OF EGG-SUCKING," or any such domestic treatise, I might jump into my subject; but "SWINDLING" is not to be approached irreverently. Its influence on the happiness of society is to be duly considered, that the maxims by which it is the hope of the author to recommend it may have their due weight upon the disciple; who, when he shall learn that swindling is, indeed, synonymous with self-preservation, will brush up his hair, take breath, and then, unless he have no more sensibility than a stock or stone, lapse into a state of the profoundest and most admiring attention. Yes; I was right—the pupil is now all ears.

Philanthropists and philosophers have come to the comfortable conclusion that there are in England too many Englishmen. John Bull has played the Sultan, and has an alarmingly numerous family. Unhappily, however, he has not the Sultan's wealth—neither has he the Sultan's prerogative: he cannot feed all his sons and daughters; he must not choke or drown them. The bow-string and the Bosphorus are not for John. What then is to become of the family of Bull? Shall they tear each other piecemeal? Forgetful of their origin, shall they destroy one another in civil fight? *Amor patriæ*—humanity—all the finer and nobler feelings of the human heart revolt at the very thought. "What," the philanthropist will inquire with tears in his eyes—"what, then, is to be done with a superabundant population?" My reply is as brief as, I flatter myself, it is conclusive— they must swindle. We have been gradually adopting what I believe to be the only remedy for the national disease; we have for some years in many instances applied what I conceive to be the only cure for the social malady; but it is only when it shall be applied upon a grand scale, when, in fact, a curative science shall be professed and practised by men cognisant of all its subtle and most bountiful capabilities—for it is yet in its infancy—that the greatness of its social value will be thoroughly manifested and acknowledged.

It is allowed that all the professions are full to running over. The Church is crammed to suffocation with applicants for deaneries, prebends, vicarages; to say nothing of the thousands with their hearts fixed upon mitres. There is hardly standing room among the candidates for lawn and silk aprons.

In the Courts of Law there are wigs as thick as cauliflowers in Battersea Gardens. Besides, the sneaking spirit of the times has so enervated the British character, that Englishmen lack somewhat of that generous pugnacity which, in the days of our fathers, would precipitate them into the arena of the law to feed with their own flesh the lions therein prowling. And when it happens that a gentleman with the true English blood in him shall resolve upon such noble sacrifice, why, so numerous are the animals awaiting him, that many a term shall pass, and not one of the *carnivora* shall have so much as a mouthful of the honest gentleman's flesh—shall not even make their mark in him. Consider it well, reader; count, if you can, the hundreds of excellent, watchful, well-disposed persons who, ev-

DOUGLAS WILLIAM JERROLD 37

ery morning during term, come down to the Courts to prey; and who, nevertheless, return to their homes all innocent of strife. Is not this a discouraging prospect for thousands of young men, most of them very willing to become Chancellor? But so it is; the profession has a greater supply than demand. In fifty years it will be thought great luck in a man to die Lord Chief Justice or Attorney-General.

In the Army, a profession that I have followed with an ardour peculiarly my own, can anything be more barren? Here am I, at the age of nine-and-thirty—I, who have—but no, the dignity of my subject, the national importance of this treatise, shall not be lessened or neglected by aught personal. Hence, I disdain to speak of a deep bayonet wound inflicted in the most dastardly manner in the small of my back, during my first campaign in Biscay—of a gash across my nose, from an enemy's sickle, when bivouacking in a henroost—of an imaginary fracture of the *os*—but no; I have said it, I will not mingle my private griefs, were I chicken-hearted enough to think them so, with matters of national interest. Besides, every man's country is proverbially ungrateful to him. Hence, I should despise myself did I more than allude, in the most evanescent way, to my heavy pecuniary losses in the service of Mexico, Chili, Peru, and other places too numerous to mention. But so it is; and what, I ask—what cares the commander-in-chief, sitting in his pride of place at the Horse Guards—what cares he for my superb plum-pudding spotted charger, shot whilst grazing—it was only the day before I had been on him—by an enemy's vidette? What cares he for the loss of my three saddles, generously given up to be converted into high-lows for my barefooted comrades? Yes, what—I must, I will ask it—cares the said commander-in-chief for the subsequent ignominy endured in consequence of that gallant steed—that by me devoted leather? Would it affect him, even for half-an-hour, to know that on my return to England—my beloved land!—after three years' absence, I was, at half-past six on a December morning, summoned by my landlady to see a Mr Jones, the said Mr Jones and a friend at the same time entering my apartment to remind me of my lost barb, my long-forgotten saddles? On that morning the commander-in-chief was, I doubt it not, snoring ingloriously in bed; little dreaming—it may be, little caring—that at that hour a brother soldier, placed between two big men in a small gig, was being conveyed at the rate of three miles an hour through fog and frost to Chancery Lane. I remember the Tyburn-like pace; for, let me do his benevolence justice, Mr Levi in the handsomest way apologised for not having had the horse *roughed*; adding that, as he had no other call to make that morning, "he was not in no 'urry."

Friendly reader, as an officer and a gentleman, I protest to you that I would not have even thus casually alluded to personal adventures did they not in the most striking, and I may add in the most pathetic manner illustrate the condition of a man who, with a military flame burning in his breast, generously offers his fire in the cause of nations. I might proceed; but the same modesty that has hitherto confined me to the rank of captain—and I may here allude to an infamous conspiracy on the part of the publisher and printers of *The Army List*, my name, as I have been informed, having been maliciously omitted from that miscellany—the same modesty ties up my tongue on my own sufferings, my own deserts; or at most but lets it move in fitful murmurings. I have done! To proceed.

In the Army what are the hopes for superabundant young gentlemen, too spirited to starve, and too nice to dig? What, I ask, can be their hopes when a hypocritic sentimentality is gaining ground amongst those who are pleased to call themselves thinking men—a whining, sneaking abuse of glory and all its mighty purposes? There is a whimpering, white-faced cowardice that would extract all the stern immortal beauty from the battlefield, showing it to be no other than a place of butchery; that would display the valiant soldier with his throat cut, his bowels gloriously protruding, as a horrible sight—a piece of sacrilege done by man upon

his fellow. And more than this, the same cant lifts up
its face of turnip pallor, and pointing to where ten or
twelve thousand stalwart fellows lie magnificently dead
in blood and mire, has the effrontery to ask *cui bono*, as
my old schoolmaster used to say—to put the impudent
"*What's the good of it?*" I should abuse the ingenuousness
of the young martial spirit were I to be silent on the
innovation of this wicked principle; a principle which,
with the infamous invention of the steam gun and the
unhallowed introduction of the rocket brigade, will go
far, or Captain Whitefeather is no prophet, to utterly
destroy what I was once proud to think the instinct for
war in the "paragon of animals." There is something
inconceivably cowardly in the steam gun. Possessed of
such engines, neither party will fight; and thus, nations
always prepared for war, will hold continual peace.
They will, so to speak, treat and deliberate at "full
cock"; and being always ready, will never fire. Is not
this, I ask, a lamentable state of the world for a man to
be born in? Let us, however, unflinchingly look truth in
the face; by so doing we shall be the better prepared for
the evil days at hand, which to enable men to meet with
some serenity of mind is the high purpose of this essay. Such days are nearer, much nearer, than those who
have capital in powder mills like to dream of. We shall,
of course, continue to keep a small standing army; but
blank cartridges for birthdays will be the only order

DOUGLAS WILLIAM JERROLD   41

from the Horse Guards: bullets will become as rare as
brilliants; whole tons of the death-dealing lead being
sold to the type-founders. Laurel, "the meed of mighty
conquerors"—why a whole grove of it will in the com-
ing time be held of no more account, nay, of not so
much, as a handful of dried marjoram. Have I dreamt
it, or did I at a late philosophical meeting see a grave,
pragmatic man rise from his seat, and when up, did I
or did I not hear him seriously put it as a motion—that
the planet Mars should be no longer called Mars, but
be known to all future generations as JAMES WATT?

The Army, then, affords no refuge for the tens of
thousands up to within these few years begotten, chris-
tened, suckled, nursed, fondled, schooled, petted, sport-
ed with, wept over by fathers and mothers, uncles and
aunts, grandfathers and grandmothers, for the glorious
purposes of war. In such case is it not, I ask, the highest purpose of the philanthropist to find employment
for men, who in happier times might have been use-
fully employed in burning the cottages of our enemies,
lessening the numbers of our enemies' children (thus
nipping a foe in the bud) on lances and bayonets, tear-
ing up olive groves, carrying away the vanity of plate
and pictures from enemies' churches, and in fire, and
blood, and terror, planting the immortal bay? Since the
British Lion is no longer to be fed upon Frenchmen's
flesh, since he is henceforth to have a regimen of bread

and milk and dates, it behoves us to see that he be gradually and duly prepared for the change in his diet, lest consumption fall upon him; or, a still greater point, lest he break all bonds and spread dismay around.

I have now, I trust, convincingly proved that the many asylums hitherto open to the pious, the wise, and the brave, are most inconveniently crammed; and that with less room for an increasing generation, the crowds will consequently become more dense, more clamorous, and in a word, more revolutionary. What is the remedy in this great natural crisis?

In one word make I answer—"Swindling!"

The philosophy of the present time is remarkable for its contempt—nay, for its wholesome abhorrence of poverty. A want of the luxuries of life is not merely inconvenient, it is positively ignominious. Hence what wrigglings, and smugglings, and heartburnings are every day acted and endured, to stand well with the world; that is, to stand without a hole in our hat or a damning rent in our small clothes! The modern man is wonderfully spiritualised by this philosophy; so much so that if he can secure to himself a display of the collar he is almost wholly unconscious of the absence of the shirt. Indeed so deep and so widely spread is this sentiment that the present time might be denominated the Age of Collars.

This spirit is on the advance; and it is the consciousness of this truth that impresses upon me the necessity of publishing a system by the adoption of which the country may be saved from a desolating revolution, and tens of thousands of future generations be secured those benefits and enjoyments which, as the sons of Adam, they are justified in expecting from the fulness of time.

I have proved, at least to my own satisfaction—a great sustaining point with an author—proved that by the natural course of things multitudes of generous spirits, before devoted to the professions, will be thrown upon their own resources—a dreadful condition for most men. What is to become of them? They cannot sink down into petty hucksters; railroads have destroyed the race of pedlars; they must not, even if they had sufficient moral courage, hold forth their white hands as medicants; and if, stung by the injustice of society, they should in a moment of exasperation take to the road, why, highwaymen, save and except the highwaymen of fifty years ago, cease to be picturesque; and there is another heavy discouragement—the barbarous institution of a rural police. These fiery souls—the unemployed, superabundant young gentlemen—must, then, become knight-errants; that is, they must institute an order of chivalry peculiar to the age, and the best calculated to meet the wants of the sufferers. Let us take a single knight.

Here is Peter Muddleton, son of Jonah Muddleton, greengrocer, Houndsditch. Jonah Muddleton dies, leaving Peter heir to the goodwill of his shop, with seven hundred pounds in the three per cents. Well, had Peter fallen upon a less ambitious age, he would have tied his apron around him, walked behind the counter, and, saving a new coat of red and yellow paint bestowed upon the outside of the shop, and the substitution of "Peter" for "Jonah," things would have gone on even as when Muddleton senior was in the flesh. Peter, however, has a spirit above ha'porths of starch and pen'orths of pepper; and having, as he most potently believes, a gentlemanly taste, resolves to do anything that may become a gentleman, but certainly not keep to a shop. The seven hundred pounds, to Peter's real astonishment, become in a brief time about eight hundred shillings. A little month and Peter is penniless. What is to be done? Is Peter to be blamed for the spirit of the age? Could he, the hapless son of a vulgar sire, stultify himself to the fascinating and exalting appeals of an advancing era? No; he is, in the first instance, the victim of over refinement, and his moral perceptions having been rendered painfully acute to the degradation of a shop, and his physical man far too thin-skinned for the labour of Adam—and, moreover, having not a sixpence, and seeing no gentlemanly mode of obtaining that much-abused yet most necessary little coin—he magnanimously resolves to eat and drink the best, and to wear the costliest, and all—without it. This is the determination of a genius: but even the most consummate wit may be assisted by the experience of others, and it would be a sorry affectation in me—it would be worse, it would be a gross injustice to my fellow-creatures—to deny that from my own observation of life I am incapable of the dearest services to young gentlemen so curiously placed as Peter Muddleton.

I have taken a single case; I have adduced one of the humblest examples; I already see a hundred thousand, many varying in their original rank in life; but all, at length, compelled by the spirit of the age to take their stand upon the broad ground of—SWINDLING.

All commercial operations of the present, and certainly of the future age, do and will tend to place the whole wealth of the country in a few hands. I am not vain enough to suppose that this book will enjoy a large daily sale for more than a hundred years; with all the partiality of an author, I cannot bring myself to expect that the state of society—whose wants the work is to meet—will endure above another century. However, I shall have done my duty, and I may safely leave the year 2000 to the active philanthropy of other WHITEFEATHERS. For more than the next hundred years there must, if my previous hypotheses are allowed, be an enormous amount of intelligence unemployed by the professions; the tangible fat of the land becoming every year engrossed by a smaller number. Now, to prevent any violent partition of property, it is—I can lay my hand on my heart and vow it—it is my purpose to make the few contribute in the easiest and pleasantest way to the wants of the many. Briefly, it is my object to show to the elegant unemployed how they may successfully and safely swindle the shopkeeping minority. The whole system is reduced into a trial of wit; and if the swindler be a man of real genius, and the man swindled have a touch of generous feeling in him, he will forget what might be vulgarly called a loss in admiration of his conqueror. I have seen much of shopkeeping nature; and I am convinced that a man properly, wholly, and withal delicately swindled—where there have been no rubs or hitches in the work—that a man who, with all his eyes and ears about him, has nevertheless, without his knowing it, been turned, "like a cheveril glove," inside out by the professor—that such a man, after the first burst of disappointment, feels but little of the bitterness of resentment; the small drop of gall in his heart is speedily taken up, and by a process delightful for the benevolent mind to consider, is assimilated to the milk of human kindness still running in the ventricles of the swindled; who—I have known such an instance—after a moody, savage look, will burst into a laugh, slap his leg, and with a confident, yea, with an exulting voice, declare that "no less a swindler could ever have swindled *him*." Here is a homage—an irresistible token of admiration—paid to one man; and if we consider, in proportion to the possessions of the others, how small, how trivial has been the tribute levied upon him, a positive enjoyment afforded to another! Believe it, reader, the swindled, if well swindled, is not without his joy.

This maxim is never to be lost sight of by the pupil. If he would disarm a man of the natural ferocity of the animal when fobbed, he must fob him blandly, graciously, completely. Humanity—a consideration of the feelings of others—demands this. How often have we seen a worthy man in a very tempest of passion—his face like copper—his eyes starting—his tongue stammering his wrongs:—"The—the—the—infamous scoundrel!—the barefaced villain! Did he think I was to be done in that way? Did he think me a fool?"

There it is, take the good man's goods; but, in the taking, see you never wound his self-love.

CHAPTER III

OF THE FACE NECESSARY TO A SWINDLER—
(AN INCIDENTAL SPECULATION ON THE "DIVISION
OF PROPERTY")—AND OF THE USE AND ABUSE
OF MUSTACHIOS

IT is a homely expression, often used in reply to a sar-
casm on a personal deformity, "that we did not make
ourselves." Not even a Professor of Political Econo-
my can argue away this conviction, rooted as it is in
the depths of the human heart. Much, however, can
be done with the rude lump—if indeed it be rude—
whereof man finds himself the ill-starred possessor.
Hence, let no one moderately deformed despair of his
fitness to join our brotherhood Hump backs, club feet,
and bow shins have, it must be owned, their disadvan-
tages for the service—notwithstanding, the genius of
their owners may triumph over such outward obsta-
cles. A fine face tastefully set in hair may be considered

DOUGLAS WILLIAM JERROLD 49

a blessing for the profession; yet it would be to inflict a great injustice on the higher uses of the science to suppose a mere face so framed all-sufficient. No; "we work by wit and not by whiskers." The outward man goes far, but he must depend upon the ethereal spark— upon the inward intelligence—for self-distinction.

And first for THE FACE OF A SWINDLER. Men who set themselves up as judges of character—I have heard the sciolists—sometimes marvel that the sons of commerce should so frequently fall victims to some individual swindler; when he, the party swindling, is one of the most ingenuous creatures breathing; looking, in fact, the swindler that he is,—when from his eyebrows to the corners of his lips there is painted in the largest human capitals the calling of the professor. The truth is, the unsuspecting men accustomed to pore over day-books and ledgers have not had sufficient time to learn to read human faces. They can on the instant, if put to the test, tell a good guinea from a bad one; but though they shall stare in the features of a human counterfeit for an hour or more, they cannot, one in a hundred, discover the washed brass from the true gold. More; though they shall hear the counterfeit—though the ring of its voice shall be the truest Brummagem—the trading man shall complacently rub his hands, satisfied that he is hearing the sweetest sound of the mint.

I confess it, to the honour of the trading communi-

ty of this commercial country, I confess it; the success
of some faces of my brotherhood upon men behind
counters has been to me startling evidence of the un-
sophisticated character of the tradesman. For instance;
there is Nobrowns, Scarceamag, Fleeceington, and others I could name—shall I own it?—I have sometimes
felt myself humiliated by their prosperity. I have felt the
science lowered by the facility with which they have in-
gratiated themselves into the favour of the jeweller, the
coachmaker, the tailor. Had *I* kept shop, I have thought
I should have shown Nobrowns to the door at the first
glance of his eye; and without looking at Scarceamag,
but simply hearing his base-metal voice, I should have
told him I had nothing in his way, and straightway
ordered him across the threshold. And yet these men
have flourished for a score of years; and, at this moment, are prosperous swindlers. How is the enigma to
be explained—how the more than Arcadian innocency
of the dwellers in Bond Street and Regent Street to be
philosophically accounted for? Is it, that men immersed
in the profound abstraction of £ s. d. lose somewhat of
the sagacity inherited and often improved by poorer
souls; that, too much rapt by the splendid visions of
the future profits, they are less vigilant as to the danger of present credit? Providence, however, hath wisely
partitioned its benefits. If it be given to Scarceamag,
with *his* face, to swindle and be poor—it is also allot-

ted to Puddingtête, the tradesman, to be swindled and
grow rich. Take this, then, my dear pupil, for an axiom:
you may—since you cannot help it—look the greatest
swindler in life; but if you shall hold your own counsel, your face shall, at least to the acute men behind
counters, never reveal it. Tradesmen can read anything
but customers' faces.[2] This truth is every day borne out
by the success of fellows whose features have gone far
to vulgarise the science. Ragamuffins who ought never
to have aspired beyond the pea-and-thimble board at
a country fair—knaves marked and impressed by the
truthful hand of nature for the lowest offices of leg-
erdemain have, trusting to the simplicity, the unsuspecting ingenuousness of a money-getting generation,
to the marvellous innocency of the commercial body,
made for themselves a reputation of the first class, or
of very nearly the first class of the highest profession.
Ultimately, in the advancement of society, these vulgar
upstarts will be met by a greater number of competi-
tors, elevated and accomplished with the graces of life,

2 I can scarcely believe that Captain Whitefeather was a reader of the Essays of David Hume; and yet a similar opinion—a friend of mine, a poor
curate to whom I showed the Captain's MS., pointed it out to me—is expressed by the sceptic philosopher, who, in his Essay on "Delicacy of Taste,"
says:—"You will seldom find that mere men of the world, whatever strong
sense they may be endowed with, are very nice in distinguishing charac-
ters, or in marking those insensible differences and gradations which make
one man preferable to another."—[Ed.]

and the term swindler will be, as it ought to be, synonymous with gentleman. The commercial faculty will, on
the other hand, be rendered more acute in its observation of human character; hence it will require a greater
delicacy of style—more imposing and a more winning
manner to arrive at any distinction—indeed, even to
make a clear paltry five hundred a year as a swindler,
than in these times will suffice to ensure to a tolerably
industrious man an income of a thousand. This is inevitable. When the tens of thousands of noble spirits,
heretofore absorbed by the professions, are left to trade
upon their wits—when all society is more strongly
marked, more arbitrarily divided into two classes, the
swindlers and the swindled—when, instead of a violent
and ruthless division of property, as infamously as ig-
norantly insisted upon by certain firebrands—there is
a graceful exchange of elegant patronage on the one
side, and a profound expression of thanksgiving respect
on the other, the character of the successful swindler
will rise to its ordained and natural elevation, and a
Whitefeather (pardon the honest vanity) take his place
with many illustrious names sufficiently obvious to the
philosophical reader. The time is happily passing away
when brute violence is to achieve national good—when
the price of bread is to be beaten down by a bludgeon,
or wages raised upon a pike. It is therefore a matter
of deep regret to the contemplative man, and such I

am not ashamed to confess myself, to perceive how many gifted persons are, by a premature nativity, ill-placed. How many men at the present day breathing national arson and patriotic pillage—men who have so profoundly studied the *meum*, that they are entirely ignorant of that of *tuum*—would, born a few years hence, have shed a lustre, have conferred a dignity upon even an illustrious and dignified profession. Let me not be asked to enumerate examples—I eschew the personal for the general. It is enough that the eye of the philosopher can perceive in many a sulphureous patriot the indefatigable swindler; that the sage, pondering on the inevitable changes of society, can detect in a present Bull-ring Brutus all the misapplied qualities of a future Isaac Solomons!

Blissful time—glorious return of the golden age—when rapine and fire, and cutting and maiming shall no longer be the evils adopted by comprehensive minds to work out, as they conceive, a great good; but when one half of the people shall live peaceably upon the other; when the whole aim and end of every two men out of four shall be to possess themselves of their daily bread—(philosophers will receive the phrase in its more enlarged meaning)—by an art demanding in its exercise the highest and most chastened faculties of the moral creature. The two halves of society will then be fairly arrayed against each other; and for ruthless weapons—for sword, dagger, and pistol on one side, and bayonet, sabre, and carbine on the other—we shall have the more peaceful and courteous instruments, silvery words, blandest smiles, and the happiest self-possession, opposed by cautious interrogation, wary looks and silent heavy doubtings. Here then is a contest worthy of intellectual beings! This is indeed a duello of the immortal principle! How poor, how savage, how unworthy of a rational creature to break into the peaceful dwelling of an honest silversmith—to fire his bed-curtains—to bruise and batter his ornate cream-jugs, his chased candlesticks, and embossed tankards,—or, the spoil carried off amidst the exulting howl of barbarians, to fling it into the hospitable melting-pot—how loathsome, how degrading this brutal mode of a division of property, to that refined and gracious system, the cunning birth of better times— the fruit of a loftier and truer consideration of man's dignity towards his fellow!

Let us consider the two pictures; let us contemplate the working of the different principles. How revolting the scene of violence! How debasing to our common nature to witness a mob of denaturalised creatures bursting in the good man's door! How they scamper upstairs! Like festal savages they wave firebrands and torches about their heads as they rush into the sacred bedroom. The worthy man says a short prayer, and

thinks of his stock—his wife and daughters, trembling
for their lives, are horrified at being seen in nightcaps
with their hair in paper! All the house is in consterna-
tion; and, a touch of humanity softening the mob, they
benevolently suffer the silversmith and his family to escape, in their night-clothes, over the roof, and descend,
like cats, into the gutter of their neighbour. The shop is
ransacked of everything; and now a sanguinary fight is
going on behind the counter between two of the ruffi-
ans for the plated top of a pepper-castor. This—this is
one principle of a division of property; as if property
was only to be divided by the blaze of torches and the
crackling of rafters! Turn we to the ennobling contrast.

Mark the swindler! How graciously he descends
from his chariot—for the swindler of first-rate genius
rarely marauds on foot—and with what a composed
elegance, with what a perfect self-possession he enters
the shop! There is something inexpressibly taking in his
manner. Surveying him from head to foot, we cannot
repress the opinion that the "age of chivalry" is *not* past.
He is the knight of later times—the Chevalier Bayard
in a round hat. *Sans peur* glows in his eyeball, and the
whiteness of his kid gloves is *sans reproche*! Two or three
centuries ago he had, with mailed hand, "shaken the
bags of hoarding abbots," and now comes he, with a
condescending smile at his mouth, to deal with a silversmith. See! he crosses the threshold—treads the shop.

It is impossible to resist the fascination of his lofty cour-
tesy. The tradesman, wary as he is—suspicious as loss
after loss has made him—despite of himself, confesses
the supremacy of the stranger, and, with a smiling lip, a
twinkling eye, folded palms, and inclined back, politely
receives his destroyer. A conversation ensues; and the
swindler—I am of course putting the case of a man of
genius—fastens upon the tradesman, who every moment becomes more deeply impressed with the consequence of his patron; and therefore, having flung to
the winds all low suspicion, is the most obsequious, the
most humble servant of the swindler. There is nothing
too costly for him—nothing too curious; no order too
difficult to be met—no time too short for the accomplishment of his wishes. The swindler is evidently a
man of the very highest consequence; and the silversmith, if I may adopt a homely expression, is inevitably
done, ay, done—

"—as brown as a berry."[3]

The swindler whirls away from the tradesman,
who has attended him, bareheaded, to the kerbstone,
and then the man of precious metals returns to his
shop in that delightful serenity of mind, apt, I am told,
to possess people with profits ranging from fifty to sev-
enty-five in the hundred.

What—it will be asked—what, does Mr Giltspur,

---

3 It will be seen that the Captain had some knowledge of Chaucer.—[Ed.]

A Polite Division of Property

the silversmith, without further questions put, trust his service of plate, besides a magnificent suite of amethysts (for which the honourable Mr Thug expressed a sudden liking), to the honour of his customer? To be sure he does; and his blood simmering with a sense of profit, he orders them to be delivered at "——— Hotel," where Mr Thug is staying; but which delightful and convenient hostelry he, shortly afterwards, suddenly leaves on the most imperative business. A thousand instances bear out the probability of Thug's success and Giltspur's discomfiture. People may talk about the innocence of a pastoral age: I am, from long experience, convinced of it, that the most innocent, the most unsuspecting, the most easily-taken biped on the face of the earth is—your London shopkeeper. Armed with proper weapons, it is almost impossible that he can escape you. The poor creature is weakness, imbecility itself; "Wear your eye thus," and as surely as the fluttering bird drops into the mouth of the snake, as surely fall the tribe of Giltspurs into the folds of the Thugs.

Well, and is it not delightful that it should be so? Here is Giltspur, for a certain number of days at least, made very happy; he has delivered his goods, and has already calculated to the odd sevenpence-halfpenny the amount of profit. Thug has conferred upon him a great pleasure—passing, it must be owned—but sweet, very sweet, whilst it endures.

Does the reader still remember the picture of violence drawn in a former page? Does he still behold the pallid silversmith—his fainting wife—and blushing daughters? Does he yet hear the roar of the flames, as they come up the staircase—the fury of pillage in the shop below?

The same effect is produced by the swindler, but how different the cause! The "division of property" is just as complete—the fine, deep philosophy that preaches it equally well honoured; and yet, what grace on one side—what civility on the other; and, to one party at least, what tangible, enduring satisfaction! Who, then, with the smallest spark of human dignity within him would stoop to violence when he may "divide" with ease? The "multiplication" of the human animal is, indeed, according to the modern school-men, "vexation"; but the "division" of property—unless divided on the bland principles of swindling—would be infinitely worse. In the progress of society, then, it is by swindling, and by swindling only, that we shall escape the most grievous revolution.

To proceed with the personal qualifications necessary to a Swindler. He must have a face of purest brass. If handsome, all the better; yet, perhaps, expression is of greater importance than the mere proportion of feature. If, however, he *look* a Swindler—if to the contemplative men who peruse human lines, printed in the

blackest ink on some human faces, he look his profession—his success with the sages of trade is certain. It
is, however, of the first importance that there should
be no alloy in the face. It should, for instance, be as
incapable of emotion as the bull hide on the shield of
Ajax.[4] This, youthful Swindler, is the besetting danger;
hence, bend all your energies to obtain a stony look
of self-possession. Though a constable should put his
"dead hand" upon your shoulder, and your very marrow should thrill at the touch—your face must remain
motionless as the face of the Apollo Belvidere—your
eye unquenched—your voice with not a crack in it. I
will not disguise the difficulties of arriving at this su-
per-human placidity. Talk of the self-possession of a
Cæsar—the coolness of a Napoleon—quackery all!
What is there in the composure of a man who takes
snuff whilst hundreds of other men's limbs are being
blown into the air (to be wept over by the spirits of
glory), with at the most a *sauve qui peut* for it; whilst, in
the scale of advantage, there is a laurel wreath and a
triumphant entry and civic addresses,—what is all this
to the quiet dignity demanded of a swindler in a peril-
ous situation—his splendid cabriolet, perhaps, waiting
at the shop—whilst, sneaked out at the back door, Bob
the apprentice has run for Police Officer Snatchem, F.

---

4 I may, by the way, observe that the Captain, whose education was not
equal to his parts, is indebted for a few of his classical allusions   to another
pen.—[Ed.]

No. 20, to attend immediately to our hero, who at his approach beholds a no dim vision of the very handsome police omnibus—the prison barber with his ignominious shears—and hears, or thinks he hears, the pathetic, admonitory address of Common Sergeant or Recorder? It may, according to a worn metaphor, take nerves of iron to direct an army; but they must be brass, and of the finest brass too, to swindle. Fighting is, indeed, a mechanic trade; millions can fight,—but how few can gracefully swindle! We know that the result of both operations is often the same, but how inferior one to the other! Bonaparte brought a *few* pictures from Italy, which the world—Heaven knows!—made noise enough about. In warlike phrase he "took them" from a vanquished people: a poor, shabby act to brag of; but had he, unassisted by squadrons and battalions, and parks of artillery—had he, by the unassisted efforts of his own mind, with no other masked battery, no other weapon than his own hand and his own tongue,—had he robbed one dealer of a Correggio—another of a Raphael—a third of a Titian—a fourth of a Murillo—and so on,—it had indeed been an achievement to boast of; but to crack of the incident as one of the trophies of the army of Italy was the sublime of gasconading! My late friend Featherfinger—he died, poor fellow, having burst a blood-vessel from intense study at Macquarrie Harbour—had a magnificent bronze clock; a superb thing! a thing to make a man value time. Had I not pledged my honour to secrecy, I could write a history touching his possession of that clock, which, of itself, is enough to immortalise any one man. My honour, however, is sacred; and my lips are hushed. This much, probably, I may be permitted to observe: The industry—nay, that is a poor, unworthy term—the genius manifested by the indefatigable Featherfinger to possess that clock—methinks I see him now; poor fellow! seated with his Greek cap, his black satin morning gown figured with pink poppies—an Indian shawl (the *gage d'amour* of an Italian countess) about his waist—his feet in bead-embroidered slippers, the work, as he protested, of some heart-devoted heiress—his meerschaum in his mouth—in his hand a book, *Satan* or the *Lives of Highwaymen* (for he was passionately fond of light literature)—his tiger page, only three feet high, and warranted to grow no taller, in green and gold, with a breast-plate of best double gilt buttons, standing at a reverential distance—whilst the bronze clock on the mantelpiece vibrated with its monitory, moralising—yes, moralising—*tick, tick!* Methinks I see him as I enter raise one eye from the page, nod, smile—and such a smile!—there was only one shopkeeper, and he was a philosophical member of the Society of Friends and dealer in *virtu*, that ever stood against it—smile, and then cast the other eye towards the clock itself with a

look of touching reproach at my delay, or with a glance
of approving pleasure at my punctuality. Methinks I
see him—Gracious powers! That such a man should
die at Macquarrie Harbour, taxed beyond his strength
of study, a victim to—but no; loyalty to the Ministry
was ever a virtue of the Whitefeathers, and I breathe
no word against the Whigs! To hurry from the theme.
Much has been said about the boldness, the fine contempt of public opinion shown by Napoleon when he
took the horses of St Mark from Venice to place them
on his own palace gate in Paris. Well, the act was not
without its merit, but did I dare to write the story of
Featherfinger's clock, the theft of Napoleon would, in
comparison to the genius manifested by my friend, sink
to the petty larceny committed by schoolboys upon ap-
ple stalls. But so it is; the finest history remains, and
ever will remain, unwritten. The Venice horses have
been celebrated by poets and historians, but posterity is left to bewilder itself with guesses on Featherfinger's clock. Yet—and I am prepared to meet the con-
sequences of such an assertion—I am convinced that
great as the conqueror was in all the varieties of the
science, Buonaparte's horses must pass from the recollection of the earth; whereas Featherfinger's clock, duly
chronicled, was a thing for time! It may be cited as an
illustration of the injustice of Fortune—of the tricks
she plays with the noble and the man—when the read-

er is informed that the tiger page of my dear friend—
of him whose bones are mouldering (for he *was* buried)
in a foreign earth—of him born, as the poet says,

> "To steal a grace beyond the reach of art—"

that that little cab-page—that tiger-moth fluttering as I
have seen him with *billet-doux* about the carriage-lamps
and round the torches of an opera night,—that he has
at this moment a country-seat and grounds at Hackney,
purchased and supported by the precarious profits of a
night-house—that is, of a mansion hospitably open in
the vicinity of Drury Lane, for the refreshment of trav-
ellers with beer, beef and oysters, from eleven at night
until six in the morning. But so it is; a genius, like my
departed friend, dies beggared at the last; whilst mere
industry at forty-five grows his own pine apples!

I have, I trust, been sufficiently minute in my description of the face requisite to be put upon Swindling.
In conclusion, I have only to enforce the necessity of
the most rigid self-discipline to prevent even the most
evanescent exhibition of what is conveniently called
modesty; for the swindler who can blush is lost. His
must be a brow whereon

> "Shame is ashamed to sit."

A money-lender, a courtier, steeped to the lips in broken promises—a pick-pocket caught in the act, all of
these may, if they can, blush and not be ruined; but

woe to the swindler whose cheek admits the self-accusing tint! His face, like the face of the man in the moon, must look down upon all sorts of acted abominations, yet blench not.

MUSTACHIOS.—These *were* pretty things for the profession; but I grieve to say it, lawyers' clerks, linen-drapers' apprentices, players out of place, and even pedestrian vendors of lucifer matches, have detracted from their exclusive importance; hence, I would counsel the youthful, sanguine swindler to eschew what indeed vulgar usage has rendered a very questionable advantage, and to swindle with clean lips. It is enough to break the heart of a rabbi to see how one of "Heaven's best gifts," the human beard, is in these hirsute days cut and notched according to the impudence or ignorance of the wearer. It is said of the French that they have a thousand ways of cooking an egg: let it be our boast that we have as many modes of dressing the chin. I have, I hope, a love of the picturesque, as the world will one day know from a work of mine still, unhappily, in manuscript.[5] I, therefore, am a passionate admirer of the beard of patriarchal growth; but for your nasty, stunted, straggly, ragged, edgy things—now like the skin of a dog with the mange, now like the end of a skein of whitey-brown thread, now as if culled from

5 *The Hand-Book of Ratcliffe Highway*, an inestimable work (when printed) for the stranger in London.—[Ed.]

chopped hay, and now as if cut from a singed blanket—pah!—were I caliph for a day—but no matter, let me not wander to legislation, but stick to my higher subject—Swindling. I say, then, to my disciple, eschew mustachios. At best they are a doubtful good. If, however, you are determined to wear them, let me hope that their hue is black as death. If, on the contrary, Heaven has awarded you a pair of pale gold or deep carrot colour, tamper not with them, but shave. Never, like Richard, think to stand "the hazard of the *die*"; if so, your case is desperate. I knew three promising young fellows, all of whom laid their ruin at the door of Mr Rowland. But—for I like to anticipate—it may be asked, Do you always, Captain Whitefeather, walk abroad with unrazored lips? To this I boldly answer that—for I was justified in the vanity—I did wear an adorned mouth; more, that a lady, who shall be nameless, was in hysterics (of course at intervals) for three days, when my mustachios fell; but no, I could not condescend to wear them when I saw—yes, I confess it—even a better pair than my own upon the face of a fellow in the Surrey gallery, selling play-bills, Spanish nuts, and ginger beer. What the revolution of society may in time produce it would of course be impudence in me, who am not a Paternoster Row astrologer, to declare; but, for the next five-and-twenty years, mustachios will, I think, be a dangerous decoration for the swindler. So much business has been done with them that suspicion will have scarcely subsided under at least another quarter of a century. The horse-tails of Ibrahim Pacha have not been more triumphant; but victory will not always perch upon the same banner.

The swindler should not at the present day hope to take the Philistines by the strength of his hair. No; let him shave, and put the barest face upon the dignity of his profession—it cannot be *too* bare.

CHAPTER IV

OF THE PARENTAGE AND NAME OF A SWINDLER—
OF HIS EQUIPAGE—OF HIS MORAL PHILOSOPHY

THE professor of our distinguished art has, it must be conceded, this peculiar and most grateful advantage—he may choose his ancestors. With the *Peerage* or the *Red-Book* open before him, it lies within his own breast to decide whether he shall have come from the loins of a Norman baron—of one of the boldest of that invincible band of marauders and thieves who jumped on Hastings beach—or whether he shall be the last of a collateral branch of the Strozzi, or Frangepani, or of any other Italian house whose beginning, in the opinion of divers heralds, dates from beyond Numa. Here is a glorious prerogative! The swindler may make his own coat-of-arms, although his immediate father walked the earth without a shirt. Show me any other man possessing so delicious a privilege. With long rolls of knights

and barons, and earls and princes before him, how the
swindler may play the epicure with the mighty dead!
How loftily, yet how serenely, may he contemplate the
titled dust of bygone generations! Even as your dainty
snuff-taker coquets with a dozen samples of the odor-
iferous tobacco, so may the swindler, pondering on a
choice of father and mother, taste with his moral sense
the various claims of buried greatness. Now, he likes
this Prince's mixture—and now this. He is puzzled,
perplexed by the hundred appeals to his filial affection.
He is one minute determined to have come from the
Montmorencys—the next, he feels a yearning towards
the Talbots—and in a few seconds, lo! he will make
a kindred to himself from the golden line of D'Este.
If the reader possess imagination—and if he do not
I tremble for my book—he must sympathise with the
delightful tumult in the swindler's brain and breast, or
rather brain alone—(for with your true swindler the
brain must have played the Aaron's rod with the heart,
swallowing it whole; a miracle very often performed in
the anatomy of great public men)—he must feel more
than commonly interested in the contest which is to
decide the parentage of our hero. With this allusion to
the delicacy of the juncture, we leave the swindler at
his books, merely impressing upon him the necessity
of choosing a long way back—of electing an ancestor from some by-way catacomb—some seldom visit-

ed cemetery—some "untrod on corner i' the earth."
Nor let him despair; there are at least a round thousand or two of dukes and princes sufficiently obscure
in their winding-sheets, albeit possibly brave and bla-
tant enough when in the flesh, from whom the swindler
may scratch out a great progenitor. All that is necessary
is that the beginner of the family shall have lived in the
dim twilight of civilisation—that he shall be so far away
that all the Herald's Colleges, with all their spectacles
upon their collective noses, shall not be able to perceive
whether the disentombed thing be flesh or phantom.
Very satisfactory progenitors have been found, with
arms to match, of thew and sinew just as questionable.
If, however, the swindler *will* have a mighty ancestor, let
him, I repeat, go far enough for him: when a man wants
a marquis, or an earl, or a count, for his great-grandfa-
ther, he should not grudge a long walk—even though
he walk blindfold and backwards—for the commodity.
So much for the ambitious swindler.

The swindler, however, who trusts to his unassisted genius, and disdains the lustre of any specious trophies from the churchyard, may with a very laudable
pride refuse to make to himself a grandfather, being
possibly contented with the grandsire selected by his
grandmother for him. Some men—and let me do all
homage to their simplicity—turn up their noses at the
genealogical tree, even though its roots were struck at

Tyburn: the swindler of sanguine spirit may be of this
proud kidney; and all the better: I augur more of his
ultimate triumph. However, though he shall refuse a
herald-begotten progenitor, it may be highly necessary
for him that he shall choose a name. His own may have
become celebrated for family achievements wide away
of his purpose; and therefore, whilst with filial affection
he sticks to his own father and mother, disdaining the
blood of Norman, Guelph, or Ghibelline—it may be
imperative upon him to assume a nominal device not
hitherto borne by any of his kin. The swindler wants a
name. Here, then, we approach a delicate, yes, a difficult point. Let me, however, set out with a solemn injunction to the swindler, that in the choice of a name
"he throw away ambition." Considerable nicety is required in the selection of a good title for swindling; a
number of fine young fellows having—if I may lighten
the solemnity of this essay with a familiar phrase—"let
the cat out of the bag" by the incautious assumption
of a high-sounding, flowery, no-meaning patronymic.
The truth is, the detestable rage for novels has so fa-
miliarised the world with a set of sugar-and-water heroes—of exquisite gentlemen, all of them worthy of a
glass case lest the flies should soil them—that their very
excess of virtue has put them on the hue and cry of
suspicion. Hence "*Delacour*," "*Erpingham*," "*Rosenthorp*,"
"*Millefleur*," and a thousand others of the courtly and

sweet-smelling class, all in their time excellent names
for swindling (that is, for swindling in the higher sense
of the term, for in "fine wire wove" they swindle still),
are now no other than brands, *stigmata*, by which the
calling of the professor is instantly suspected. Hence,
my dear pupil, take no sweet, pastry-cook name from a
novel; cull no flower from a play-bill; but look, as either
a poet or a member of Parliament says, I forget which,
"look abroad into universality" for the thing desired.
As you walk the street cast your eyes above the door
of the worthy shopkeeper. A thousand to one that in a
day's saunter you will possess yourself, and from such
a source, of a name in every respect unexceptionable.
Yes, from the board of the thriving, honest, painstaking, till-respecting tradesman. And if so, how inge-
nious, how pleasant withal, to obtain one of your best
weapons from, so to speak, the armoury of the enemy,
to be fleshed immediately upon him! It is perhaps unnecessary to warn the young swindler that he must not
be too homely in his choice. There is a class of names
which, from their very abundance, makes it a matter
of constructive ignominy to swindle under them. And
some of these are Jones, Walsh, Welsh, Thomson,
Johnson, Dobson, White, Brown, Williams, Simp-
son, Smithson, and that multitudinous monosyllable,
Smith! If, in a moment of hilarity you break a lamp,
wrench off a knocker, or snap a bell wire, why any one

of these names may be, as of course every gentleman well knows, confidently given in to the night constable; but to attempt to swindle under them betrays a petty larceny spirit in the professor, from which my experience looks for little present gain or future reputation. No; the name of a swindler should be like the wardrobe of the true gentleman—a thing not challenging vulgar attention; but, if examined, found to be of the very best material and of the choicest workmanship. Hence let the swindler choose between a *clinquant* (I do believe this is almost the first bit of French appearing in the essay, for the which I confess myself deficient in the graces of modern literature[6]), between the *clinquant* of novel heroes and the homeliness of "base mechanics"—let his name be a solid, substantial, downright English name.

I say English, for I think we have had too long a peace to render the assumption of a foreign title and a foreign accent worth the trouble, the incessant watchfulness, the continual stretch of a man's intellects: the call upon his faculties to keep up the character should be well rewarded, for the hazard of self-discovery is very great. I know a remarkable instance of the danger. There was Thaddeus Ballynamuck—he once, with

---

6 The Captain is in error. Though his essay is, assuredly, barren of "the tongues," the author knows more of bookmaking than he apparently chooses to confess.—[Ed.]

merely a backward touch of his hand, broke the jaw of the manager of a minor theatre who dared to offer him terms to bring him out as a Patagonian giant—there was Thaddeus, who had made a splendid six weeks' campaign at the West-end as an Italian count; how admirably did he with the *lingua Toscana* flavour his native Connaught! The Duke of Tuscany was his dear friend; and not without reason; for Thaddeus at a boar hunt had stood between the boar and the duke, receiving the tusks of the beast in his hunting jacket, for the which he had obtained a great many Italian orders, and on the strength of which he gave a great many English ones. Well, Thaddeus, though considered as true an Italian as the poet Asso,[7] was one morning driven to the necessity of shaving himself, changing his southern name, and retiring for a few weeks to the privacy of Southend. He was betrayed into self-discovery by an excess of benevolence—the more was the pity. Thus it was. He always carried in his cab a beautiful dove-coloured Italian greyhound, its legs not much thicker than goose quills, and its tail like bent wire—the gift of the Marchesa di Lungabarba. The dog had leaped from the cab and followed its master into the office of Finings, the wine merchant. Thaddeus had before very considerably patronised Finings, and was about to give him a splendid order for some choice port to

---

7 The Captain doubtless means Tasso—[Ed.].

be shipped to his friend the duke—and how the eyes of Finings twinkled at the title of his highness!—when the cellarman, a brawny, heavy fellow from Somerset, shambled into the office and trod, with all his fourteen stone, upon the delicate toes of Angelo the greyhound: the dog howled with agony piercing enough to crack the parchment heart of an old maid, when the Captain—he was, at the moment, with the greatest difficulty endeavouring to make himself understood to the wine merchant—turned round, and, to the astonishment of Finings, fulminating a string of oaths in the very purest Connaught, dealt a blow on the breast of the cellarman that sent him prostrate on three dozen of choice brandy—picked samples for the dowager Lady Drinkwater—to their utter destruction, and to the exceeding surprise of the wine merchant, who had never in all his life heard an Italian count vituperate such beautiful, such unadulterate Irish. I will not continue the story: Thaddeus Ballynamuck, though an admirable artist, fell a victim to the exuberance of his feelings; as a swindler he was professionally killed by Angelo, the late Marchesa di Lungabarba's greyhound.

I have narrated this little history that it may serve as an illustration of the perils besetting an honest, simple, guileless Englishman who might wish to swindle as an exotic. There is, it must be allowed, unnecessary peril in the experiment; besides I question if it be not

Perils of a Foreign Accent

unpatriotic. Why defraud our mother country of the advantage of our reputation? Why, with ungrateful, with unfilial hand add a leaf to the laurel of Germany—of France—of Italy—of Russia? No; for a true born Briton to swindle as a noble from the Hartz mountains—as a count from Paris—a Roman count—or a prince from St Petersburg—is poor, shuffling, shabby, or, if I may use a term which I am proud to find of late very current among politicians and political writers (for the classes are more distinct than people are prone to imagine)—it is *Un-English*.

America, however, has her claims upon us. The swindler may, and with profit, prove his recollection of the ties that once bound Columbia to Britain—may gratefully acknowledge a sense of the relationship between the mother and the daughter country, by swindling as a gentleman with enormous possessions in New York, or, what is still better, in Virginia. Here the many-sided philosopher cannot fail to recognise a new advantage in a community of language. The *soi-disant* (hem! French again!), the *soi-disant* American swindler may avenge the injuries of a greyhound on the person of a cellarman, yet run no risk of discovery. He may still run up and down the gamut of execration and not betray himself. Think of this, youthful swindler. Besides, there is another great temptation to offer this passing honour to America. Her unsettled

currency affords the swindler a hundred plausible ex-
cuses if—for such improprieties do occur at the London Hotel, Grillon's, the Clarendon, all the very best
of houses—if rudely pressed to show those credentials
of gentility which even the rudest and the most illiter-
ate never fail to acknowledge. Thus the swindler may
for a time throw himself upon the banks: and this the
more safely if he have displayed a handful of letters of
introduction (a few to the royal household), all easily
manufactured, and all, for the time, as good as letters
of credit. There is another very practicable deceit. He
may, on the night of his arrival in London, have his
pocket picked of certain Government securities, and,
having made the keeper of the hotel the depository of
his secret, straightway advertise the loss in all the papers. This, I confess, is a ticklish experiment, demanding the finest self-possession, the greatest delicacy to
carry it into successful operation; and if the youthful
swindler have any doubts of himself, I charge him by
his hopes of future profit and reputation not to think
of hazarding it. Should he, however, succeed, and the
landlord advance liberally, he may condescend to express his best wishes for the prosperity of his host, and
more, may invite himself to dine with him. Great cau-
tion, however, is to be used before there be any advance
to such familiarity; and yet I once knew a gentleman
from Natchez who obtained unlimited credit from his

host—the pot-house keeper was musical—by insisting
upon it that he made Dibdin's *Lovely Nan* by the very
force of expression remarkably like Rossini. So far, all
was well; but, forgetful of what was due to himself as
a swindler,—in the genial atmosphere of a domestic
hearth letting himself down to the level of his host—
the foolish fellow suffered himself to play at cribbage
with his landlord; a man who had spent at least half of
his long and useful life, pegging. Game after game the
landlord's doubts increased: and at length he rose from
the table with a blank in his face, and all the swindler's
bill in his heart. "I'm done—I know I'm done!" cried
the host with a groan. "I must be done, for no true
gentleman could ever beat me at cribbage." At least
one month's board and lodging, besides the greatest of
all advantages, the first-rate reference to shopkeepers,
did my friend from Natchez lose by his skill at cribbage. It is true when hard pressed he talked a great deal
about the last failure of the cotton crop—an excellent
theme, by the way—but in this case he talked to the
winds, or, what was much worse, to a man obstinate
upon his bill. My friend had to make an ignominious
retreat, leaving behind him all his goods generously
subscribed for him by the ingenuous West-end shopkeepers. Notwithstanding this, the swindler may for
a time take America for his country. The trick is by no
means over-done. If, however, the swindler make the

election—if he resolve upon becoming a gentleman of enormous fortune from the United States—he had better choose the South, and, above all things, he must not forget the cotton crop. As it once happened at New Orleans, much execution may, even in London, be done upon the enemy from behind cotton bags. As for his rank, the swindler should not venture beyond that of colonel—yes, a colonel and a great grower of cotton.

We next come to a most important subject—the dress of the swindler. The present age judges of the condition of men as we judge of the condition of cats—by the sleekness, the gloss of their coats. Hence, in even what is called a respectable walk of life, with men of shallow pockets and deep principles, it is of the first importance to their success that, if they would obtain three hundred per annum, they must at least look as if they were in receipt of seven. Very many stoical privations are endured for this great purpose. How many a fine hungry fellow carries his dinner upon his back—his breakfast in his beaver—his supper in his boots! The Hottentot is not the only human animal that clothes itself with the cost of bowels. The swindler, however, is not—fate forbid that it should be so!—called upon to make the same sacrifice required every day in London of the poor, friendless student—of the miserable, unknown artist—the juvenile surgeon, panting for a practice—the barrister, without a fee—the curate, with lips hungering for even locusts and wild honey—the thousands of God's most helpless creatures, gentlemen, born with a silver spoon, but left by fortune at their maturity without any employment for knife and fork—no, no, it is the purpose, the triumph of swindling to put its professors in purple and fine linen, and to make "their eyes red with wine and their teeth white with milk." They have to dress well, not to keep up the barren name of gentleman, but to flourish as swindlers. Poor Dactyl, the poet—astonishing truth!—is too proud to take credit for a hat—too poor to buy one—and too high-spirited to nod to his old college friends in a rusty beaver. Will the reader listen to a fact? What does Dactyl? Why, he makes a compromise with his magnanimity—he over-persuades himself that his beaver is as yet tolerably jetty, since all the summer he has once a day sponged it with a damp sponge, and kept religiously upon the shady side of the pavement. I mention this wretched shift of a pusillanimous spirit to show to the young swindler what might be his fate if, with a pertinacity only found in simpletons of the very first class, he would resolve to live the gentleman upon the revenue of the chameleon; and, with not a sixpence in his pocket, would be sufficiently mad to rave about honour in his bosom. What is the reward of such obstinacy—what the goal of men so honourably idle—so perversely pure? What the end? Go,—ask it of the Thames! Put the question to the Serpentine—the New River—the canals! Mutter the query as you pause at the gunsmith's—as you linger at the chemist's! Ask, as you see whisk by you the chariot of the coroner!

I had not touched upon this mean-spirited class of bipeds—of the species, many of whom die off in honourable poverty, and many in a dishonourable horse-pond—did not swindling save a third portion of the body from a life of starvation and an end of vulgar misery. The good, indulgent parents who, in submission, as they conceive, to the high civilisation of the day, will rather let their sons be nothing if they cannot put them in a fair way to become archbishops, chancellors, and commanders-in-chief, owe much to swindling, for—urbane goddess!—how often does she take the pet of the fireside—the darling of the chimney corner—the pretty prodigal, when plucked of every feather by the jackdaws[8] of the town, and make of him again a bird of finest plumage. Yes, thousands and thousands of young gentlemen, shamefully deserted by their parents when they had not a farthing more to leave them, and—wanting a calling—with nothing to do, have been received with open arms by the tenderest of foster-mothers; and not only once more set upon their legs, but, perhaps, for the first time in their

---

8 I persuade myself that Captain Whitefeather here meant nothing personal.—[Ed.]

lives, put into their own cabriolets! Little thinks the
plodding tradesman, determined upon making Tom a
gentleman, that his dear boy may owe all the external
appearances of that character to nought but swindling.
But I have wandered.

The swindler must dress well—very well; nay, he
must be rather over-dressed than under-dressed. If his
means be scanty, he must on the outset, if I may use
the phrase of a celebrated bill discounter, late of the
New Cut—he must "spend his money superficially";
that is, as the before-named fiscal authority condescended to explain, he must expend a little in such
a way that the outlay may appear very considerable.
He must, however, continually bear this in mind,
that in this our beloved country—in England—the
empress of nations—the queen of reason—the genius of toleration—and the benefactress of the op-
pressed—nearly everything depends upon a man's
coat. Great and rich is he indeed who can afford to
confront the midday sun in threadbare cloth. It matters not what may be your genius—what your worth;
you must make the success of that genius apparent—
you must publish the reward of that worth; you must
assure men's eyes that you are a fine gentleman, or
you will, with all your glorious aspiration, be passed,
confounded with the mob. The triumphs of mind are
to the trading million too subtle, too abstract, to be

easily grasped; but the quality of a man's coat—the gorgeousness of his vest—the chain of finest carat— the ring of brightest sparkle—all of these are so many indisputable evidences of worldly success, and are, therefore, to be continually carried about by a man as universal vouchers for his character. John Bull has certainly the largest eyes of any of the nations. Hence, if it be imperative upon men with even a known call- ing to exhibit an outward sign of the prosperity of that craft, how much more is it incumbent on us—the minions of Mercury, with nothing but the vivacity of our wits "to feed and clothe" us—to put a splendid outside upon swindling, and since the world ducks to appearance, to assure ourselves of its very, very low- est stooping! I have never yet known an instance of a successful swindler in a shabby coat. Who, indeed, would trust a man with a hole in his hat? Read the Po- lice Reports—those "short and simple annals"—how, nineteen times out of twenty, do they commence? Why, thus—"Algernon Mountedgecomb, a young man dressed in the highest style of fashion," etc., etc. Such is always the strain; for can the reader point out any case with any verbal similarity to the follow- ing:—"Yesterday, John Snooks, a wretchedly attired fellow, was brought up charged with obtaining under false pretences a diamond ring, a gold repeater, and a suit of pearls from the house of——?" Has ever such a case been chronicled? Certainly not: hence, the tailor is indispensable to the swindler, who is on no account to spare him. The swindler may, in the weakness of his nature, have some qualms towards any one except a tailor; but the swindler who deals mercifully with a tailor had better seek another profession—such chicken-heartedness is not for our art. The benevolence is so much goodness lost—wasted—flung to the winds; for you are to bear with you this recollection: it is an axiom in his trade, that the tailor never loses. "Them as does pay"—such was the confession of an eminent coatmaker after his second bottle of Burgundy drank at Button Park, his country seat—"them as does pay," said the good man, "pays for them as doesn't." Can there be a finer provision for the protection of trade, and the satisfaction of the non-paying? Hence, if possible, flay your tailor. Should he discount—for there are such philanthropists—let him have a few bills by all means. In his vast profits what are two or three thousands more or less in a twelvemonth's balance? *If*, however, he will not discount the paper of your friends—"accommodate" is a good word—he cannot refuse your own bill. Great is the satisfaction of a bill! What serenity comes upon a man's soul when he hath writ "accepted"! What a load he feels lifted from his lightened heart! How airily, how joyously he looks around him, elevated with a sense of duty done to his neighbour and to himself! Sweet, most sweet, the satisfaction! Such I am sure was the feeling of my late lamented friend, Captain Judas Gammon; for that excellent fellow never accepted a bill that he did not clasp his hands and, raising his eyes with a devout look of thanksgiving, exclaim, "There now—thank heaven—! that's paid!"

There is, however, one objection to a bill—it puts another pair of wings to the back of Time. Hence, get a long day. He was a philosopher and knew human nature, and more than all, those profound workings of the human heart set going by the machinery of bills,—he *was* a sage who, at the Old Bailey bar,—what men of wit and genius have made that nook all classic ground!—having received sentence of seven years' retirement from the bustling world, thus, with smiling face, addressed the judge:—"I beg your pardon, my lord, but have you a stamp about you? if so, permit me to accept a bill at seven years, for then they'll pass like one."

Next for equipage. A swindler, like a physician, can scarcely hope to prosper on foot. He must *ride* to fame and fortune: hence a cab is of the first consequence to him. This, however, is too obvious to call for further disquisition. The effect of a magnificent cab—a grey blood—and a diminutive fancy tiger—upon the sensibilities of the shopkeeping world are every day made manifest by the Police Reports. Jonathan Wild, Richard Turpin, and other worthies laboured on horseback—civilisation adds to their less bloodthirsty descendants the comforts and the graces of a cab.

And now, come we to the moral bearing of the swindler. Destiny has marked him to play a very various character. He is, I will not attempt to disguise it, beset by difficulties. There are men, assuredly, born with a genius for the profession; who, as it would seem, instinctively adapt themselves to all its peculiarities; men who would have been lost, sacrificed, utterly unknown in any other calling. I do not address myself to them—this luminous work is not written for their instruction; but to the thousands of the rising generation, induced, tempted, by the spirit of the times—a spirit of the most tyrannic gentility—to live without means; to eat the fat of the land without once greasing their delicate fingers in search of it. Let these, however, not conclude that our path lies over flowers: by no means; there are very many rubs to be endured on the way—rubs calling for at once the greatest self-possession and the most admired meekness. Indeed, I should not discharge a great public duty did I not state it as my conviction that very far less powers of mind, and ingenuity of a much lower scale, are found sufficient to make a fortune in any of the low mechanic arts of life than are required by even the humblest swindler. However, the ardour of youth is not to be withstood; hence our best choice is to instruct and fortify it.

And now, neophyte swindler, let me put a few questions to you. And ere you answer, submit to a most rigorous self-examination—search every hole and corner of your heart; and then hold up your head and reply unblushingly.

Can you bear what is called public contempt? Are you clothed with a moral armour, more impenetrable than the scales of the dragon—from which the glances of reproach, the scoffs, the sneers, the hard abuse of vulgar minds—the mere pity of those prigs who call themselves philanthropists—shall fall aside unfelt and unremembered?

Can you school yourself to look in all human faces—for this trial *will* come—and find them blank?

Have you sufficient fortitude to witness unrepiningly the good fortune of some early companion—a dullard, yet plodding, and what the world calls honest—surrounded with all the luxuries of life, the fruits of lowly huckstering, when, possibly, you yourself are yearning for a tester?

Can you bear with the nerves of a martyr the visitation of a horse-whip—for I will not shirk any of the probabilities that wait upon the profession—or the vindictive and un-Christianlike application of a pointed boot to the *os sacrum*?[9]

Can you, at proper time and season, bear your nose pulled? I am aware that this is perhaps the most difficult, the most trying ordeal for the weakness of human nature to withstand; and therefore, I repeat the question—Can you bear your nose pulled?

Can you, with no qualms at your throat, behold in rags or in a gaol the simple gull who has trusted you, or who—more exquisitely simple still—has become your surety?

Can you, when old age approaches, and your place in the world is filled up by more active, more youthful professors—can you, with your hand upon your heart, retire like a philosopher to a corner, and with not an eye to look comfort to you, not a lip to breathe hope to you, not a hand to grasp your hand—can you breathe your last breath with the conviction that you have done no injury to the dead, will leave no wounds in the living—and that having passed a life in heroic defiance of

9 "It is very strange," remarks Captain Whitefeather in one of his unpublished essays, "On Personal Satisfaction," "how very few men know what is due to themselves and to the second party, in inflicting what they call personal chastisement. I have," continues the Captain, with that delightful ingenuousness which made him the soul of his circle, "I have been kicked, horsewhipped, cudgelled, tossed in a blanket, pumped upon and flung into a horse-pond, yet I never, but in one instance, met with a man who thrashed me *like a gentleman*?"—[Ed.]

human prejudices, you meet death with the magnanimous indifference of a roasted Indian?

Consider, my dear pupil, whether you are so happily organised that you can support these trials—too often attendant on our chivalrous profession—and answer.

The pupil laughs at the impossibility of such evils, and, chuckling at the fun, says—I can.

And Swindling takes him to her arms and makes him all her own!

CHAPTER V

A BRIEF SUMMARY OF THE ADVANTAGES
OF SWINDLING

I HAVE, I hope, made it sufficiently plain to the plainest understanding that the faculty, the desire to swindle, is born with us, and that it is entirely owing to the force of circumstance whether we swindle or not; and that, however nice, and moral, and exemplary, we may be in our individual capacity, swindle we must and do, when we congregate together, even with what are termed and considered the very best intentions. This being granted, let every man with all possible speed enroll himself as one of a body corporate. He may be a most rigid member of a Temperance Society, considering the parish pump the only source of all human enjoyment; and yet, as one of a body, he may drive a very pretty trade in opium. He may, to his great self-exaltation, hold a plate in aid of the funds for the dissemination of the true faith; and yet the diamond on his finger may have been purchased with an odd balance of the profits which, as one of a company, he receives from a Hindoo idol. What the superficial world denominates and brands as swindling in the individual it applauds as spirited speculation, wisdom, foresight, a fine knowledge of business in a number. Hence, if a man would swindle safely, steadily, and above all, respectably, let him become one of a public company, and his dearest wish is straight fulfilled. What a profound liar he may be on the Stock Exchange, and yet what an oracle of truth at his own fireside! How he is permitted to rob his neighbour by means of false intelligence, and what a roaring he is justified in setting up should some famishing, unprincipled scoundrel lessen by one the numerous tenants of the good man's hen-roost! Reader, if you are not already enrolled, become one of a body. Though you may be only able to edge yourself into a vestry, it shall be something. And what a relief it is for the individual man, compelled to walk half his time through the world in tight moral lacing, to be allowed to sit at his ease at the Board! If morality sigh for leisure, where can it be enjoyed if not in a company! Once in a company, how many Catos become Antonys!

To the rising generation the advantages of swindling are incalculable. The term swindling is, at present, an ugly one; but with the advancement of the world it will be considered as another and a better system of ethics. To obtain all things needful for the refined man, by the exercise of the moral faculties, is, doubtless, the greatest triumph of human intellect, and this is inevitably achieved by the successful practice of swindling.

There is another advantage—another consolation—that I have purposely left for consideration in this place.

When the plodding, sober, thrifty man quits this noisy world—made noisy by the incessant rattling of pounds, shillings, and pence—it is ten to one that he makes what is generally called an irreparable gap in a large circle of the most affectionate of friends. He leaves a widow broken-hearted—daughters inconsolable—sons in the deepest affliction—nieces and nephews very much concerned—and innumerable acquaintances all ready, with very little further excitement, to burst into tears. Now here is a woe inflicted upon fifty people by the decease of one man—yes, here are fifty people made more or less miserable by a very natural event, the decease of a worthy soul, who would not willingly inflict a moment's pain upon any living thing.

How different the death of the swindler! He makes no irreparable gap in society—not he! he agonises neither man, nor woman, nor child; not a tear is dropped at his grave—not a sigh rises at the earth rattling on his coffin! Must not the conviction of this be the sweetest consolation to the dying swindler? Think of his end, and——

    *   *   *   *

    *   *   *   *

[It may be thought that the work ends abruptly. It does so: the author had not leisure to finish it. The following letter will, perhaps, throw some light upon the matter. It was addressed by the Captain to an intimate friend.

"H.M. Transport, Barrington.

"DEAR TOM,

"We are off for blue water. Some papers of mine are in a deal box in the two-pair back of the Bag-o-Nails. If you love me, see I'm in print. I learn from a fellow-shipmate—whose only misfortune is that his handwriting was very similar to another gentleman's—that the papers will make a very pretty book, there being a great call nowadays for the greatest information in the smallest compass. You can pay in for me what you get through the Home Office. Be wide awake, and believe me, under all convictions,

                        "Yours truly,

                "BARABBAS WHITEFEATHER.

"P.S.—You know I never liked shaving; the chin's bad enough—but   when it comes to the head, it's 'regular cruelty to animals.'"

The above is ("errors excepted") a true copy of the Captain's letter. He died in—I regret to say I cannot give the exact latitude: suffice it to say he died; but left behind him what, I trust, will prove an imperishable monument of his social worth and his exalted genius.]

THE EDITOR'S CHAPTER TO THE READER

THE reader has, probably, marked a variety of style in the foregoing pages. The Editor feels it to be due as much to the lamented Captain Whitefeather as to himself to state that he, John Jackdaw, is solely responsible for the manner in which this work is presented to all the eyes of the British public.

Nature had been very prodigal to the Captain; but whether from the extreme vivacity of his genius, or whether from a more hidden cause, it is vain to search, the Captain, with all his debts, owed nothing to art. Even his orthography was of the happiest originality.

The Editor, therefore, felt the peculiar delicacy of his task. Had he printed the MS. as it came, with the bloom upon it, from the Captain's hand, it was to be feared that in this age of light reading—which reading, like pills, is made to be bolted, not, like bread, to be carefully chewed—not one out of a hundred would have had the necessary patience to go through with it.

To suppress the work for any defect of style would have been to sacrifice, as the Editor considered, a great national good. After much deliberation there appeared to him a golden mean. It struck the Editor that he might, in very many instances, give the style of Whitefeather, whilst in very many more he might heighten, and adorn, and vary it from his own poor resources. Still, be it understood, all the *facts* are Whitefeather's; the Editor only lays claim to certain tropes, and metaphors, and inimitable felicities of expression, to which, probably, it might be considered indelicate were he more emphatically to allude. Indeed, he has only touched upon the theme in the way of business; as there may be, even at this moment, many noble and distinguished authors who, "wanting the accomplishment" of grammar, are yet desirous of appearing in print. (To these, in parenthesis, the author addresses himself; assuring the tadpole *literati* that he finishes tales, histories, biographies, poems, etc., with all despatch, and with the most inviolable secrecy. His address is in a former page, and Breakneck Steps is too well known to all who would mount Parnassus.)

To the publishers of the remains of Captain Whitefeather the Editor has to express his warmest gratitude. The Editor blushes for the intelligence of the trade, when he states that this national work, like the hitherto inimitable *Robinson Crusoe*, was offered in the humblest

manner to twenty houses, and, sometimes coldly, sometimes sulkily, sometimes indignantly refused.

One was tickled by the title, but looked blank
when he understood that there was no murderer—no
highwayman in it. He declared that the only way to
keep a reader awake was to commit at least one mur-
der in every page; that the gallows was now the only
bay tree, and that even the youthful generation sucked
intelligence and morals from tales of the gibbet, with
the same eagerness and the same advantage that they
sucked liquorice root! "Season it, sir—season it," said
one bland gentleman, "with a handful of murders—a
terrific storm on the New River—and a miraculous escape from Marylebone watchhouse, and there may be
some hopes of it." A second asked me to change the
title into "THE HAND-BOOK OF THE MONEY-MARKETS,"
adding, to my astonishment, that he had no doubt the
staple of the matter would serve equally well. A third—
but why should I enumerate the rebuffs endured? No;
let me rather, in the name of an obliged generation,
register a gratitude to the enlightened spirit under
whose auspices the book appears—a work destined, as
the Editor with all diffidence declares, to work a good
as incalculable as, perhaps, unknown!

ALSO FROM
CURIOUS PUBLICATIONS

The Practical Magician and Ventriloquist's Guide
by Anonymous

Mircale Mongers and Their Methods
by Houdini

The History of Spiritualism (Vols. 1 & 2)
by Sir Arthur Conan Doyle

Psycho-Phone Messages
by Francis Grierson

*Spectropia, or Surprising Spectral Illusions
Showing Ghosts Everywhere*
by J. H. Brown

Spirit Slate Writing and Kindred Phenomena
by William E. Robinson

How to Speak With the Dead: A Practical Handbook
by Sciens

*The Talking Dead: A Collection of Messages from
Beyond the Veil, 1850s-1920s*
Edited by Marc Hartzman

The Book of Dreams and Ghosts
by Andrew Lang

curiouspublications.com

www.ingramcontent.com/pod-product-compliance
Lightning Source LLC
Chambersburg PA
CBHW022104020426
42335CB00012B/816